GREEN POEMS

For Ann South

OXFORD
UNIVERSITY PRESS

Great Clarendon Street, Oxford OX2 6DP

Oxford University Press is a department of the University of Oxford.
It furthers the University's objective of excellence in research, scholarship,
and education by publishing worldwide in

Oxford New York

Athens Auckland Bangkok Bogotá Buenos Aires Calcutta
Cape Town Chennai Dar es Salaam Delhi Florence Hong Kong Istanbul
Karachi Kuala Lumpur Madrid Melbourne Mexico City Mumbai
Nairobi Paris São Paulo Singapore Taipei Tokyo Toronto Warsaw

with associated companies in Berlin Ibadan

Oxford is a registered trade mark of Oxford University Press
in the UK and in certain other countries

Text copyright © Jill Bennett 1999

The moral rights of the author have been asserted

First published 1999

British Library Cataloguing in Publication Data available

ISBN 0-19-276197-8 (hardback)
ISBN 0-19-276198-6 (paperback)

Typeset by Mary Tudge Typesetting Services and Melissa Orram Swan
Printed in Hong Kong

GREEN

GREEN POEMS

Collected by Jill Bennett

OXFORD
UNIVERSITY PRESS

Contents

sad or happy?

tomorrow's now

one world,
one home . . .

I Like the World

I like the world
The world is good
World of water
World of wood
World of feather
World of bone
World of mountain
World of stone.

World of fibre
World of spark
World of sunshine
World of dark
World of raindrop
World of dew
World of me
and
World of you.

Steve Turner

Who Am I?

The trees ask me,
And the sky,
And the sea asks me
Who am I?

The grass asks me,
And the sand,
And the rock asks me
Who am I?

The wind tells me
At nightfall,
And the rain tells me
Someone small.

Someone small
Someone small
   But a piece
   of
   it
   all.

Felice Holman

You and I

Only one I in the whole wide world
And millions and millions of you,
But every you is an I to itself
And I am a you to you, too!

But if I am a you and you are an I
And the opposite also is true,
It makes us both the same somehow
Yet splits us each in two.

It's more and more mysterious,
The more I think it through;
Every you everywhere in the world is an I;
Every I in the world is a you!

Mary Ann Hoberman

A Song

I am of the earth and the earth is of me.
I am all the colours of the corn field,
   and the corn field
    is all the colours of me.
I am all the colours of the ploughed–up garden,
   and the ploughed–up garden
    is all the colours of me.
I am of the earth and the earth is of me.

We are together under the blue sky.
We are together under the yellow
   sun.
We are together under the grey
   clouds.
We are together:
   sisters

Arnold Adoff

One Light, One Sun

One light, one sun,
One sun lighting ev'ryone.
One world turning,
One world turning ev'ryone.

One world, one home,
One world home for everyone.
One dream, one song,
One song heard by everyone.

One love, one heart,
One heart warming everyone.
One hope, one joy,
One love filling everyone.

Raffi

Presents

What will you give me
     to shake and shine?
Cherry blossom
     and celandine.

What will you give me
     that's white and red?
Daisies, that put themselves
     to bed.

What will you give me
     seven times over?
Buttercup, dogrose,
     cowslips, clover . . .

What will you give me
     of green and blue?
Earth and sky
     and the ocean, too.

Jean Kenward

where *wild things grow*

Green

I like green.
Yes.
Green is a growing colour:
dark, in the slate-grey shadow
under the trees,
brighter than sunshine,
paler than larch and lichen . . .
Green has a million faces.
When a breeze
shivers the grasses
so that they twitch and tremble
a million different pigments mix
with these—
but they're all of them green.
Green is a magic colour.
D'you think there's a green somewhere
that nobody sees?
A new one, freshly born
in the dew of the morning,
stolen by fieldmice
out of the podded peas?

Jean Kenward

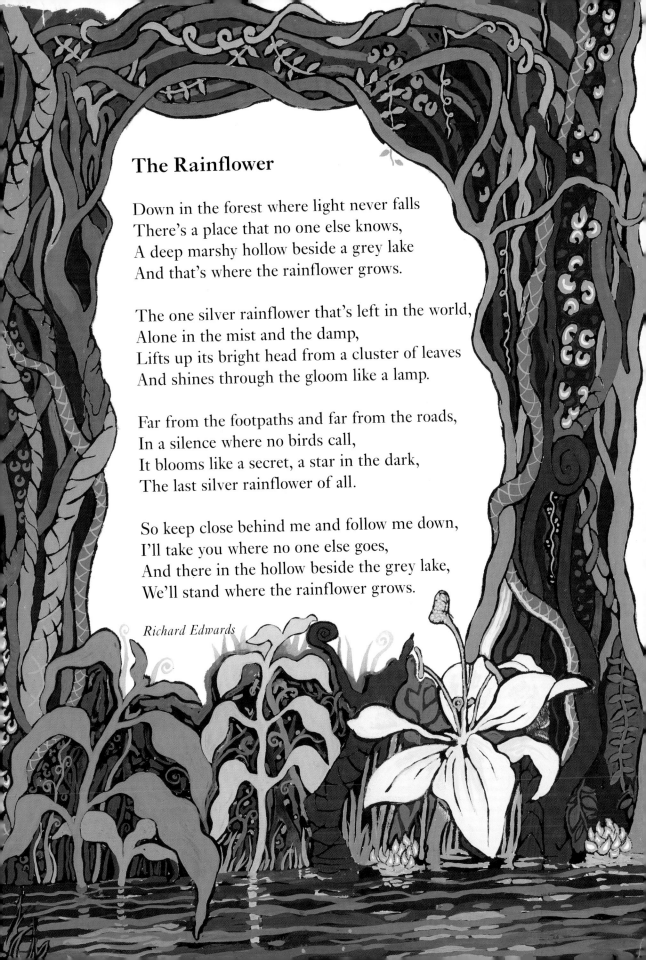

The Rainflower

Down in the forest where light never falls
There's a place that no one else knows,
A deep marshy hollow beside a grey lake
And that's where the rainflower grows.

The one silver rainflower that's left in the world,
Alone in the mist and the damp,
Lifts up its bright head from a cluster of leaves
And shines through the gloom like a lamp.

Far from the footpaths and far from the roads,
In a silence where no birds call,
It blooms like a secret, a star in the dark,
The last silver rainflower of all.

So keep close behind me and follow me down,
I'll take you where no one else goes,
And there in the hollow beside the grey lake,
We'll stand where the rainflower grows.

Richard Edwards

Seed Spell

Bury me dark,
bury me deep.
Let me lie
awhile, asleep.

Let my root
stretch out, uncoil,
sifting goodness
from the soil.

Let me push
my small shoot where
it reaches up
to light and air.

Leaves uncrinkle,
one by one,
soaking up
the rays of sun,

so that soil
and light and air
help me grow,
at last to bear

a flower that brings
the fumbling bee
to store bright pollen
at his knee . . .

and so the flower
becomes a fruit
that holds a seed
that grows a shoot

which, helped by soil
and sun and rain,
begins the cycle
once again,

as life goes slowly
round and round
on Nature's strange,
amazing ground.

Tony Mitton

Two Owls

I'm keeping my eye on a baby owl,
Who's keeping his eye on me,
I found him deep in the woods today,
At the foot of a very tall tree.

'He must have fallen a long way down,
But if you look up you'll see
Why he's quite all right where he is,' said
    Dad,
'And I think we should leave him be.'

So I looked up high and I saw two eyes
At the top of that very tall tree,
The baby owl's mum was staring down—
Keeping an eye on me!

June Crebbin

Quiet Things

Hush! I'll show you quiet things—
moon and stars and a barn owl's wings
speckled moth on mottled sill
white mare standing paper-still
gap-toothed gravestones, hollow trees
flat-roofed fungus colonies
coins and bones long buried deep
hedgehog hunched in spiny sleep.

Sue Cowling

Butterfly

This morning I found a butterfly
Against my bedroom wall.

I wanted to hold it,
To remember its colours.

But instead I guided its whirring shape
Towards the open window.

I watched it drift into the warm air,
Swaying and looping across the summer garden.

In my book I found:
'Tortoiseshell, reddish orange with yellow
   Patches.'

But I remember its leaving,
And the pattern of its moving.

June Crebbin

Fawn

Pine needles fall
To the forest floor
Lining it
In deep piles
Of soft brown.
Sunbeams push
Through crowded leaves
Of tree-giants
Scattering dazzling drops
Of white
Upon the ground.

Deep in the forest
A newborn fawn
Lies hidden,
Its body, soft and brown
As pine needles,
Its back sprinkled over
With spots of white
Like shimmering drops
Of sun.

Curled up in a hollow
By its mother,
The fawn rises
On slender legs,
Noses in and out
Among the shadows,
A silent, newborn
Dappled patch of forest.

Beverly McLoughland

Nightbird

Long after dusk
rain is falling.
Streetlamps lit.
Pavements wet
with yet more rain.

Cars are moving
through the town.
Wheels splashing.
Wind lashing
leafless trees of winter.

The church clock
strikes at nine.
Stained-glass windows shine
into the night.
A blackbird settles. Sings.
With all his might.

Ann Bonner

Drought

Remember rain?
Those first drops
that hit the dusty earth?

When empty sky
always blue
shows not a single cloud

you think of rain's
thirst-quenching smell.
The water on the rose.

Ann Bonner

Blue Magic

In the woods the bluebells seem
Like a blue and magic dream,
Blue water, light and air
   Flow among them there.

But the eager girl who pulls
Bluebells up in basketfuls
When she gets them home will find
   The magic left behind.

Eleanor Farjeon

Treecycle

We planted up the old dump,
In November with young trees,
Just two feet tall,
No leafy wall a-swaying in the breeze.
And Sam, our cheerful leader, said,
'Step back! Now this is true,
Just close your eyes for sixty years,
There's a forest in front of you.'

Ian Larmont

Be Different to Trees

The talking oak
To the ancients spoke.

But any tree
Will talk to me.

What truths I know
I garnered so.

But those who want to talk and tell,
  And those who will not listeners be,
Will never hear a syllable
  From out the lips of any tree.

Mary Carolyn Davies

if we're not careful

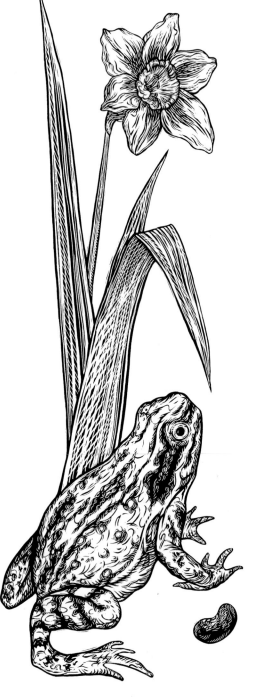

Nature's Alphabet

A for an apple.
B for a bean.
C for a caterpillar
plump and green.

D for a daffodil.
E for an egg.
F for a frog
with a springy leg.

Over the Earth
there's an ABC
of living and growing
on leaf and tree.

If we're not careful
we'll get to Z
and find the whole alphabet
dry and dead.

Tony Mitton

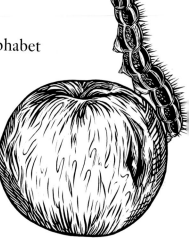

Who Made a Mess?

Who made a mess of the planet
And what's that bad smell in the breeze?
Who punched a hole in the ozone
And who took an axe to my trees?

Who sprayed the garden with poison
While trying to scare off a fly?
Who streaked the water with oil slicks
And who let my fish choke and die?

Who tossed that junk in the river
And who stained the fresh air with fumes?
Who tore the fields with a digger
And who blocked my favourite views?

Who's going to tidy up later
And who's going to find what you've lost?
Who's going to say that they're sorry
And who's going to carry the cost?

Steve Turner

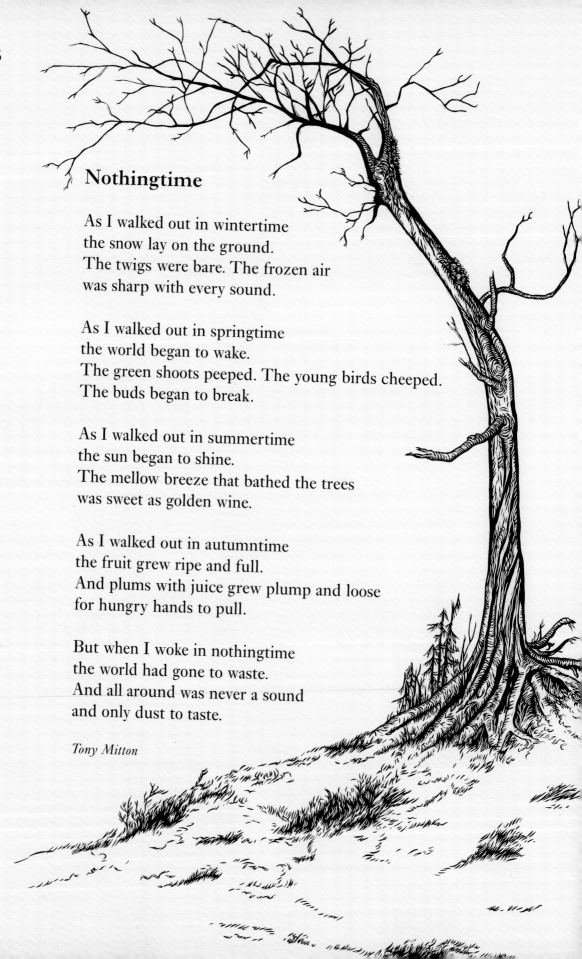

Nothingtime

As I walked out in wintertime
the snow lay on the ground.
The twigs were bare. The frozen air
was sharp with every sound.

As I walked out in springtime
the world began to wake.
The green shoots peeped. The young birds cheeped.
The buds began to break.

As I walked out in summertime
the sun began to shine.
The mellow breeze that bathed the trees
was sweet as golden wine.

As I walked out in autumntime
the fruit grew ripe and full.
And plums with juice grew plump and loose
for hungry hands to pull.

But when I woke in nothingtime
the world had gone to waste.
And all around was never a sound
and only dust to taste.

Tony Mitton

Television News

While we take burgers, Cokes, and fries
The TV tells of hate and lies
Shows death beneath bright foreign skies
Can someone pass the salt?

The ground is parched, the river dies
The Red Cross camp has no supplies
The cold night air is cut with cries
Which ice-cream have you bought?

With bones stuck out like blunted knives
And bellies swollen twice the size
The people cling to fading lives
Who's washing up tonight?

We see their pain in bulging eyes
And faces gaunt and thick with flies
The camera zooms as someone dies
What's on the other side?

Steve Turner

Sensible Seed

A seed lay sleeping
under the ground.
It gave a little quiver
and had a feel round.

It gave a little shiver
and put up a shoot.
It gave a little wriggle
and put down a root.

The root took a sip
at the deep dark soil.
'Funny,' said the root,
'it tastes like oil.'

'Yes,' said the shoot,
'and this is no joke.
The air up here
smells just like smoke.'

So the root and the shoot
both quietly agreed
to go back to sleep
in their safe little seed.

Tony Mitton

Five Fat Bluebells

Five fat bluebells,
Chubby buds galore,
One's flattened in a press
Then there are four.

Four fat bluebells
Underneath a tree,
One's picked and tossed aside
Then there are three.

Three fat bluebells
Drinking in the dew,
One's battered by a stick
Then there are two.

Two fat bluebells
Standing all alone,
One's trampled by a boot
Then there is one.

One fat bluebell
Fading in a jar—
Go back to the beginning
And leave them where they are!

Sue Cowling

Ready, Steady—Moo!

It's peaceful here by the river,
All by ourselves in the sun,
Having a chew and a chat now and then,
Moving gently along.

But I'm not too keen on the hikers
That pass through our field each day,
One of them always waves a stick
In a menacing kind of way.

I'm not too keen on their children
Dashing all over the place,
Or their dogs, which run and nip at my heels
And yap in front of my face.

If only they'd just keep going,
If only they'd leave us alone,
Don't they know they're walking through
The middle of our home?

It's time we taught them a lesson,
Yes, but what can we do?
We could try giving voice to the way that we feel:
Ready, steady—MOO-OO-OO!

It's peaceful here by the river,
Now that the hikers have gone,
All by ourselves in the meadow again,
Flicking our tails in the sun.

June Crebbin

River Song

Water laps, laps
at the river's edge,
watched silently
by grass and tree.

Water flows, flows
beyond the banks,
a tireless traveller
to a distant sea.

Judith Nicholls

River

The river is rushy,
The river is deep,
The river has fishy
Secrets to keep.

The river is khaki,
The river is still,
The river has murky
Pockets to fill.

The river is eerie,
The river is dead.
The river has scary
Rumours to spread.

Sue Cowling

The Soldiers Came

The soldiers came
and dropped their bombs.
The soldiers didn't take long
to bring the forest down.

With the forest gone
the birds are gone.
With the birds gone
who will sing their song?

But the soldiers forgot
to take the forest
out of the people's hearts.
The soldiers forgot
to take the birds
out of the people's dreams.
And in the people's dreams
the birds still sing their song.

Now the children
are planting seedlings
to help the forest grow again.
They eat a simple meal of soft rice
wrapped in banana leaf.
And the land welcomes their smiling
like a shower of rain.

John Agard

Black Smoke

Black smoke, black smoke,
blowing in the air.
Dirty rain, dirty rain,
messing up my hair.

If all the cars were quiet
and all the chimneys clean,
I would be the prettiest child
that you have ever seen.

Black smoke, black smoke,
blowing in the air.
Dirty rain, dirty rain,
messing up my hair.

Robin Mellor

Grey and White and Black

They've changed our living spaces
To grey and white and black.
What used to be our wetlands
Are concrete and tarmac.
Where once a stretch of water—
A motorway, or worse,
A man-made, hard-core desert,
An antiseptic curse.

Where once a thriving reed-bed,
A place to rest and feed
When winter time was over,
A place to stretch and breed,
Is now a dry, hard greyness,
No vestige of a lake.
It won't come back . . .
No more tarmac,
For everybody's sake.

Ian Larmont

Tree-Kill

Chip chop
Chip chop
Down comes a tree

Chip chop
Wallop plop
Help, it's fallen on me!

Chip chop
Chip chop
Down comes another

Chip chop
Wheee! bop!
That one fell on mother

Chip chop
Chip chop
Crush on daddy's head

Chip chop
Please stop
Or else we'll *all* be dead!

Spike Milligan

sad
or happy ?

Sad or Happy?

What is sad?

A cat on a chain
pacing round and round
and longing to be free.

A fish in a tank
with nowhere to go,
a lonely chimpanzee.

What is happy?

A cat on the plain
who can pace and prowl
and pounce and wander free.

A fish who can dive
and glide and slide
beneath the silver sea.

A chimp who can climb
and clamber high
around his favourite tree.

A cat who can purr
and lick her lips . . .
Then taste her favourite tea!

That's happy!

Judith Nicholls

New Life

Springtime.
The light lingers
a little longer
in the evening sky.

Springtime.
Tiny seedlings
unfold green leaves
to the sun.

Springtime:
and the blossom
is like laughter
in the trees:

for the dead of winter
is defeated.

Lois Rock

1998 Year of the Ocean

'Plenty of fish in the sea'

Save the ocean,
Save the sea.
Keep it clean and
sewage free.

Don't want oilslick's
filthy trail.
Save the seabird.
Save the whale.

Dolphin friendly
tunafish
makes an eco-
tasty dish.

Is there plenty
in the sea?
Not too greedy
must we be.

See the seashore
pure and wide.
No more Coke cans
on the tide?

Hear the ocean.
Heed its plea.
Spare the ocean.
Save the sea.

Ann Bonner

Leave the Whales Alone, Please!

Leave the whales alone, please,
They don't do any wrong;
They swim in every ocean,
And fill them with their song.

Leave the whales alone, please,
Like us, they've got a brain;
But if we don't start using ours,
We won't see them again.

Leave the whales alone, please,
We need them in the seas;
We need their life and beauty,
And all they need is peace.

Leave the whales alone, please,
Let them live their lives,
Let them leap, and swim, and sing—
Let the whales survive!

Tony Bradman

Fish Farm

Swim salmon swim,
Inside the prison net.
You'll never swim the open sea,
My plate is all you'll get.

Ian Larmont

Dolphin Dance

We are darters and divers
from secret sea-caves.
We're divers and gliders,
we dance through the waves.

We spiral and curl,
we weave as we fly,
stitch shimmering arches
from ocean to sky.

Judith Nicholls

Gorilla . . .

has a mouth
like a watermelon inside.

Teeth like seeds
when he yawns.
Eyes

like a coal black
old pit stack
smouldering there.

Did he stare?
Did he glare?

He makes me afraid.

Strange worlds in his look.
And his coat

dark as night
with bright

equatorial

stars.

Ann Bonner

Wolf

Unmoving,
like a dark stone
on a white lawn,
he stands alone.

Body alert,
ready to run back,
the last wolf scout
of the last wolf pack.

He watches for signs
of danger everywhere,
next time you look
the wolf might not be there.

Robin Mellor

Open All the Cages

Open all the cages,
Let the parrots fly—
Green and gold and purple parrots
Streaming up the sky.

Open all the cages,
Let the parrots out—
Screeching, squawking parrots swooping
Happily about.

Open all the cages,
Set the parrots free—
Flocks of parrots flapping homewards
South across the sea.

Silent trees in silent forests
Long for parrots, so—
Open all the cages,
Let the parrots go!

Richard Edwards

Lion . . .

is lying on the bank
where grass no longer grows.
His tangled, shaggy mane
frames his sad head.
His tail flicks now and then
at pestering flies.
He yawns.
Contemplates the cloudy skies.

Were you king, lion?
Once upon a distant time
were you king of the drumming
hot and humming beating bush?
The endless yellow plain?
Were you king of your domain?

And now, lion.
Beneath these windy chestnuts
your queens, your lionesses still
prowl, pace this piece
of limited English space
as if to kill.
Growl, lion. Stand,
once grand lion.
The keeper brings your dinner.
Eat your fill.

Ann Bonner

The Elephant Child

Under an African sun he stands,
the elephant child,
hot and hungry and thirsty.
He's as big as a car
but still small for an elephant.
Sadly swinging his trunk he stands
for many hours beside his mother,
trying to coax and nudge her back to life
to take him home.
He could not help her when the men came.
They just laughed at him.
And now
under an African moon he stands
and tries to make sense of her butchered face.
Then he cries as only an elephant can cry
but he does not understand.
Neither do I.

Sue Cowling

Looking at an Elephant

That elephant is
unbelievably
big
enormously
huge
wondrously
wide
tremendously
tall

while I
am decidedly
small.

Ann Bonner

Tame Bear

Bears in a circus,
bears wearing chains,
bears bearing blisters
dancing in pain.

Bears in prison pits,
bears begging food,
bears biting other bears,
bleeding from wounds.

Wild Bear

Bears in the bushes,
bears in the trees,
bears scoffing mice and frogs,
gobbling grass and leaves.

Bears fishing rivers,
bears killing seals,
bears on other bears
picking off fleas.

Gina Douthwaite

The Monkey

More skilful
Than any acrobat,
The monkey
Swings himself
Across the cage,
Then sits, bored,
Staring at the visitors
Who offer food
He does not need
And urge him
To perform tricks
He does not want to do.

What a performance
He would give them
In the forest's trees,
If only he were there!

John Foster

If I was a Bird . . .

If I was a bird
I would like to fly in the sky
so that everyone could see me.
I could fly in and out of the clouds and caves.
There'd be just one pest in my life—
that's a man with a gun to shoot me,
Him I wouldn't like.

If I was a man and not a bird,
I'd never shoot at birds
because a bird is lovely to see
when it's flying.
If I was a man I'd just watch,
not shoot.

Anon.

The Nest

Snick! go the shears. Snick! Snick!
There's a man there, cutting the hedge;
he's making it straight as a railway line,
with a string to mark the edge.

But what's that bulge in the middle,
so dark, in the heart of it?
I think there's a blackbird, sitting . . .

He's not going to cut that bit.

Jean Kenward

The Old Man in the Park

The old man's here again today
on his bench by the chestnut tree,
sharing his crumbs
with each sparrow that comes,
letting them land
on his skinny brown hand,
smiling and talking
and nodding his head
at the little brown birds
that are sharing his bread.

Sheila Simmons

Plea to an Enthusiastic Mini-Beast Collector with Magnifying Glass and Match Box

Leave me be!
I'm no c
  r   e-c
    e   i   r
      e p   a
             w   e—
               li

some day soon I'll
unzip this knitted coat
and soar away on silk
screen-printed wings.

Don't bug me!

Moira Andrew

The Cabbage White Butterfly

I look like a flower you could pick. My delicate wings
Flutter over the cabbages. I don't make
Any noise ever. I'm among the silent things.
   Also I easily break.

I have seen the nets in your hands. At first I thought
A cloud had come down but then I noticed you
With your large pink hand and arm. I was nearly caught
   But fortunately I flew

Away in time, hid while you searched, then took
To the sky, was out of your reach. Like a nameless flower
I tried to appear. Can't you be happy to look?
   Must you possess with your power?

Elizabeth Jennings

tomorrow's
now

Today's Tomorrow

Today the seed—
Tomorrow the grain.
Today the planting—
Tomorrow the gain.

Today's now—
Tomorrow's then.
Today's children—
Tomorrow's men.

Tonight's darkness—
Tomorrow's light.
Tonight's blindness—
Tomorrow's sight.

Today's sword—
Tomorrow's plough.
Today's decisions—
Tomorrow's now.

Pat Moon

I am a Tree

I am a tree.

Like you
I breathe,
I reproduce.
I too need the warmth of the sun,
The wetness of the rain,
The space to grow.
One difference between us two
Is that
You need me
More than I need you.

Pat Moon

Dreamer

I dreamt I was an ocean
and no one polluted me.

I dreamt I was a whale
and no hunters chased after me.

I dreamt I was the air
and nothing blackened me.

I dreamt I was a stream
and nobody poisoned me.

I dreamt I was an elephant
and nobody stole my ivory.

I dreamt I was a rainforest
and no one cut down my trees.

I dreamt I painted a smile
on the face of the Earth
for all to see.

Brian Moses

Recipe for a Dragon

Take hot chilli peppers
numbering three,
add four cups of sulphur
and the sting of a bee.

Rub two sticks together
to make smoke and spark.
Borrow breath from a glow-worm
who lights up the dark.

From a winter bonfire
lift the heart of an ember
to put with some leaves
from fiery September.

Place all the ingredients
in an old metal pot,
ignite with a sunbeam
and stir up the lot.

Just when you're thinking
that nothing will happen,
out of the white steam
will come a small dragon.

Robin Mellor

When the Sun Rises

When the sun rises, I go to work,
When the sun goes down, I take my rest,
I dig the well from which I drink,
I farm the soil that yields my food,
I share creation, kings can do no more.

Anon. Chinese 2500 BCE

My House

My house is not my house
if there's someone without a house
alongside my house.

The thing is that my house
can't be my house
if it's not also the house
of whoever has no house.

Anon. Cuba

I'd Like to Squeeze

I'd like to squeeze this round world
into a new shape

I'd like to squeeze this round world
like a tube of toothpaste

I'd like to squeeze this round world
fair and square

I'd like to squeeze it and squeeze it
till everybody had an equal share

John Agard

Making the Countryside

Take a roll of green,
Spread it under a blue or blue-grey sky,
Hollow out a valley, mould hills.

Let a river run through the valley,
Let fish swim in it, let dippers
Slide along its surface.

Sprinkle cows in the water-meadows,
Cover steep banks with trees,
Let foxes sleep beneath and owls above.

Now, let the seasons turn,
Let everything follow its course,
Let it be.

June Crebbin

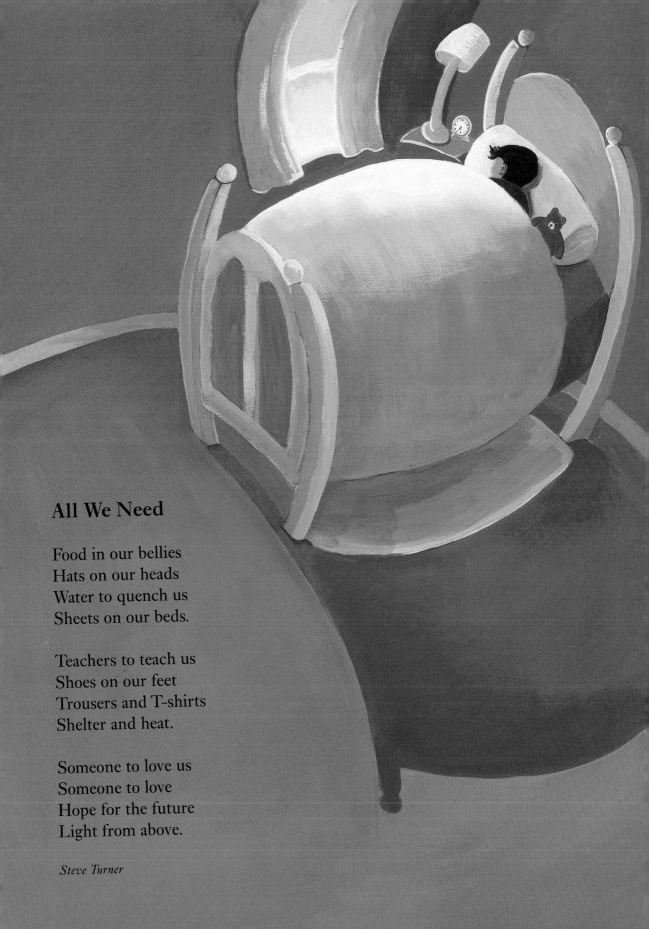

All We Need

Food in our bellies
Hats on our heads
Water to quench us
Sheets on our beds.

Teachers to teach us
Shoes on our feet
Trousers and T-shirts
Shelter and heat.

Someone to love us
Someone to love
Hope for the future
Light from above.

Steve Turner

Index of Titles and First Lines

(first lines are in italic)

Index of Authors

Acknowledgements

We are grateful to the authors for permission to include the following poems, all of which are published for the first time in this collection:

Ann Bonner: 'Lion', 'Looking at an Elephant', 'Gorilla', 'Plenty of Fish in the Sea', and 'Nightbird', all copyright © Ann Bonner 1999; **Sue Cowling**: 'River' and 'Five Fat Blue Bells', both copyright © Sue Cowling 1999; **John Foster**: 'The Monkey', copyright © John Foster 1999; **Jean Kenward**: 'The Nest', 'Green', and 'Presents', all copyright © Jean Kenward 1999; **Ian Larmont**: 'Fish Farm', 'Grey and White and Black', 'Treecycle', all copyright © Ian Larmont 1999; **Robin Mellor**: 'Recipe for a Dragon', 'Wolf', and 'Black Smoke', all copyright © Robin Mellor 1999; **Tony Mitton**: 'Nothingtime', 'Nature's Alphabet', 'Seed Spell', and 'Sensible Seed', all copyright © Tony Mitton 1999; **Judith Nicholls**: 'Dolphin Dance', 'Sad or Happy?', and 'River Song', all copyright © Judith Nicholls 1999.

We also acknowledge permission to include previously published poems:

Arnold Adoff: 'A Song', copyright © Arnold Adoff, from *All the Colours of the Race* (Lothrop Lee & Shepard). **John Agard**: 'The Soldiers Came' from *Laughter Is An Egg* (Viking, 1990), copyright © John Agard 1990; 'I'd Like to Squeeze' from *Get Back Pimple*, (Viking, 1986), copyright © John Agard 1986, both reprinted by permission of the author c/o Caroline Sheldon Literary Agency. **Moira Andrew**: 'Plea to an Enthusiastic Mini-Beast Collector With Magnifying Glass and Match Box' from *My Red Poetry Book—A Coloured Bridge* edited by Moira Andrew, (Macmillan Education, 1988), reprinted by permission of the author. **Ann Bonner**: 'Drought' from *Infant Projects No. 92: Deserts* (Scholastic, 1993), reprinted by permission of the author. **Tony Bradman**: 'Leave the Whales Alone, Please!', copyright © Tony Bradman 1991, first published in *Monster Poems* edited by John Foster, (Oxford University Press, 1991), reprinted by permission of The Agency (London) Ltd. All Rights Reserved and enquiries to The Agency. **Sue Cowling**: 'Quiet Things' and 'Elephant Child' from *What is a Kumquat*, (Faber & Faber, 1991), reprinted by permission of the publisher. **June Crebbin**: 'Butterfly', from *The Dinosaur's Dinner*, (Viking, 1992), copyright © June Crebbin 1992, reprinted by permission of the author; 'Making the Countryside', 'Ready, Steady Moo!', and 'Two Owls' from *Cows Moo, Cars Toot* (Viking, 1995), copyright © June Crebbin 1995, reprinted by permission of Penguin Books Ltd. **Mary Carolyn Davis**: 'Be Different to Trees' from *The Earth is Painted Green* (Scholastic, 1994). **Gina Douthwaite**: 'Wild Bear, Tame Bear', copyright © Gina Douthwaite 1993, first published in *An Armful of Bears* edited by Catherine Baker, (Methuen Children's Books, 1993), reprinted by permission of the author. **Richard Edwards**: 'Open All The Cages', copyright © Richard Edwards 1992, from *Moon Frog* (Walker Books, 1992), and 'The Rainflower' copyright © Richard Edwards 1986, from *The Word Party*, (Lutterworth Press 1986, Puffin Books, 1987), both reprinted by permission of the author. **Eleanor Farjeon**: 'Blue Magic' from *The Children's Bells*, copyright © Eleanor Farjeon 1957, reprinted by permission of David Higham Associates. **Mary Ann Hoberman**: 'You and I' from *My Song is Beautiful*, copyright © Mary Ann Hoberman 1994 (Little Brown & Company, 1994), reprinted by permission of the publisher. **Felice Holman**: 'Who Am I', copyright © Felice Holman 1970, from *At The Top of My Voice And Other Poems* (Scribners), reprinted by permission of the author. **Elizabeth Jennings**: 'The Cabbage White Butterfly' copyright © Elizabeth Jennings 1997, from *A Spell of Words* (Macmillan Children's Books, 1997), reprinted by permission of David Higham Associates. **Beverly McLoughland**: 'Fawn' copyright © Beverly McLoughland 1993, from *A Hippo's Heap* (Boyd's Mills Press), reprinted by permission of the publisher. **Spike Milligan**: 'Tree-Kill' copyright © Spike Milligan Productions 1981, from *Unspun Socks from a Chicken's Laundry* (Michael Joseph, 1987), reprinted by permission of Spike Milligan Productions. **Pat Moon**: 'Today's Tomorrow' and 'I Am A Tree' from *Earthlines* (Pimlico, 1991), copyright © Pat Moon 1991, reprinted by permission of the author. **Brian Moses**: 'Dreamer' from *Hippopotamus Dancing and Other Poems*, (Cambridge University Press, 1994), copyright © Brian Moses, 1994, reprinted by permission of the publisher and author. **Raffi**: 'One Light, One Sun', words and music by Raffi, copyright © 1985 Homeland Publishing (CAPAC), a division of Troubadour Records Ltd. All Rights Reserved. Reprinted by permission of Troubadour Records Ltd. **Lois Rock**: 'New Life', copyright © Lois Rock 1997 from *Glimpses of Heaven*, (Lion Publishing, 1997), reprinted by permission of the publisher. **Sheila Simmons**: 'The Old Man In The Park', copyright © Sheila Simmons 1988, from *My Violet Poetry Book—Where Wild Things Grow* edited by Moira Andrew, (Macmillan Education, 1988), reprinted by permission of the author. **Steve Turner**: 'Television News', 'All We Need', 'Who Made a Mess?', and 'I Like The World' from *The Day I Fell Down the Toilet* by Steve Turner, (Lion Publishing, 1996), copyright © Steve Turner 1996, reprinted by permission of the publisher.

Although every effort has been made to trace and contact copyright holders before publication, this has not been possible in every case. If notified, the publisher will be pleased to rectify any errors or omissions at the earliest opportunity.

Artists

Cover illustration by Alison Jay
Richard Pargeter, pp. 6–11
Jenny Cockram, pp. 12–23, and endpapers
Vanessa Card, pp. 24–35
Caterina Perestrello, pp. 36–53
Clare St Louis Little, pp. 54–61